T0063995

The Drops of Dew

The
Drops
of Dew

Revelations of the Rhythms of Life

BHUPESH CHANDRA KARMAKAR

PARTRIDGE
A Penguin Random House Company

To order additional copies of this book, contact
Partridge India
000 800 10062 62
orders.india@partridgepublishing.com

www.partridgepublishing.com/india

Dedication

I would like to dedicate this book to my son Kamal who is constant inspiration in my life.

Part I

Preface

To seek a verbal outlet to the pent up emotions comprising of the rainbow of experiences is a distinctive tribute to the sensitive self of an artist. The present collection of poems presented by Bhupesh Chandra Karmakar consisting of 306 different pieces, it presents a mosaic of twin colors of joy and pain reflecting the various dimensions of human experiences. Variety, sensitivity, experimental tones, suggestive ease is some of the key features of the each unit that is like precious pearl consisting of its own beauty. The cumulative output of them is to inculcate the sensibility among the human being against the existing ordeal of life.

I hope the present collection will be a milestone in the rich galaxy of Indian English poetry.

Poet deserves my good wishes and congratulations.

16 December 2014   sd/-
                                          (Dr. Beena Agarwal)
                                          D. S. College, Aligarh

Contents

1

A Prayer

O Lord,
Let my heart play your song-
Let me sing of your beauty,
Let me offer you my heart.
O Lord,
As bird sings and the wind blow,
My heart also craves to pray you,
O Lord
Give me awareness to call thy name.

2

A Destination

When I desired to lit a big candle,
It gives me an un-bearable trouble.
When a pretentious problem arise,
For unseen calamities I surprised.
It makes restless and impure mind,
Which needs the sensation to find?
Even if it is impression but not illusion,
O Lord it leads to destination.

3

The Christmas

A pleasurable-
Rhyme rings a bell in the ear,
As because the-
Christmas is round the corner.
It is the time-
To welcome nicely a new year,
And to fascinate-
The mix of old and newcomer!
The New Year is-
The time for all the memories,
In a delight we-
Lighted up, even the bakeries.
As the season-
Of puja we feel joyous & cheer,
In the Christmas-
It diminishes the barriers
It enlightens the soul and unites the body.

4

Friendship

Tide may come tide may go.
Fashion may come it may go.
But friendship will never go on.
Even to say color may fade,
Delicious taste may change,
But friendship will stay.

5

Affection

Money cannot give happiness and affection,
May it produce the material satisfaction!
When the children are in a good environment,
The joy comes those delightful moments!
He, who gave us the sense of satisfaction,
In precious moment wants to offer affection!

6

Harassed-Soul

He, who while-
Eating, drinking and walking,
Could not forget-
His wife but kept remembering.
He, who's always-
Praying to the great Almighty,
For his wife-
Whom he never thought guilty!
He, who always-
Agrees to sacrifice pleasure of life,
Never spends his-
Time to search his bosomed friend!
To satiate his-
Ambition he chooses to sacrifice,
But his harassed-
Soul finds nothing to rejoice.

7

Cheerful appearance

Do not deceive anybody-
Do not despise any one,
Anger will only harm in turn.
Let your love spread beyond borne of family,
Without hatred and anger take each one gaily.

8

Blossomed Flower

I live as I please-
Even I feel always pleasure,
I move as I like-
Because my heart is clear.
I felt happy-
When I visited this nice land,
It was like my native-
Place, like a beautiful island.
She also looked happy-
In the boat into flowery river,
Changed her frame of-
Mind like a blossomed flower

9
A writer

I could not be a good writer,
Nor could I be communicator.
My writing style may be perfect,
But unable to express the fact!
In the literature and in quality,
I felt lack of discerning ability.
I desired to be all times writer,
Make my words, the voice of our times.

10
Happiness and Joy

As the blessed person enjoying life,
He desired to share happiness and joy.
As God always gives His best to us,
Happiness never depends on others.
Happiness is the celebration of soul,
It is the reflection of divine.

11

My Mother

I love my sweet-
Mother who was my instructor,
By the mercy of
Her I am bliss enlighten other.
My mother who-
Taught me Vedic conclusion,
Even guides me-
About all other's nice religion.
Her explanations-
Reduced my all the ignorance,
Self consciousness-
Are symptoms of soul's presence?

12

My Wife

As sky is nothing without cloud,
Garden is nothing without flowers
Grass is nothing without nice dew
My life is a weed without my wife.

13

Spiritual Preceptor

He, who is having good judgment,
I could feel through his argument.
He inspired me in spite of ignorance,
And removed my feelings of darkness!
In my life he will be a teacher,
Will always act like spiritual preceptor.

14

Beam of Sun

Do not feel disappointed or frustrated,
As ego is self-imposed or self created!
If nature of moon is an effect of mind,
Beams of sun act for enlightenment.

15

My daughter

O my sweet daughter,
You filled home with laughter,
As silently you sleep —
Happiness becomes deep.
In the beautiful home-
You can peep to see moon.
And make all shinning-
When from dark moon is emerging!

16

God's Gift

When it will be a dawn, the sweet birds will sing.
God gave very rich land and fruitful tree to save.
When birds come to you, never allow flying away,
Every purpose there is a time to lead happiness.

17

A Melancholic Love

It was really a fantastic beginning,
When met in fragrance of evening.
None would protect or even ask,
As it would become absolute dark.
We broke silence of environment,
As though lived in a tinny planet!
We might travel in the big ocean,
Where our love born in a season!
Though our affairs emerged in sun,
But like a butterfly that had flown.
A period arrived like grain of sand,
In critical situation we had danced.
O, my love become a pattern of music,
Brings it neither joy nor melancholy.

18

God's Presence

God is like sweet fragrance,
Like the scent of an incense,
Being person of innocence,
I always realize his presence.

19

Bliss of Joy

He, who encourages,
To face all the confusions,
Got light and won an illusion.
He, who proceeds towards,
Success of nice path,
May be called a very wise person!
He, who attains,
The spirit of self-realization,
Always feels bliss of joy and satisfaction.

20

A Beautiful Life

One needs to have control over emotions.
Though poets gaze there for inspirations,
He, who remains always extremely cool,
Obviously can lead his life bountiful!
If life is harder in perishable environment,
Let us not make it harder in excitement.

21

Peacock Dance

There was no-
Boundaries of my happiness,
Though I was-
In deep forest and felt loneliness?
As from a distance-
Happily I saw peacock dancing.
The rustle sound-
Of wind over trees was flowing.

22

My Mom

My mom, who joyfully adored Almighty,
Was pleasingly cleaver and talked smartly.
She, who graced through look sheepish,
Created blissful environment to cherish!
Through the process of transformation,
She took various shapes like bird, Swan.
She, who transformed the beam of a light,
As like as a Karina Yogi she also sat alight.

23

A Thought

They, who were bright, highly educated,
Tried to follow up for the career they bred.
They immersed in the joy of developing,
As the life is too short to worth living!
The young were abandoning business,
It was due to lack of self-consciousness.
In the village there was magical silence,
They desire glass of eggnog with appliance.
In change of season with joys and worries,
They realized the thoughts, hope and tears.

24

Welfare

Through a good and through a bad-
Through a delight and through a sad-
I think depression was a good past,
Nothing left for future or present.
God is always in my life I realized,
In child's sweet smile, the fulfillment I realized.

25

A Teacher

Teacher is-
The revealer of high values,
Who points out-
The defect or mistake with reason!
He never tries-
To compare with luxury of teaching,
Who provides-
Sound reason to do the something!

26

An environment

When person become-
A patient in a moment of anger,
His thoughts of the-
Bitterness is nurtured in mind.
When a person planting-
The mango saplings in the garden!
It become a tree and-
Absorbed heat from surroundings!

27
Mother's Inspiration

An inspiration emerged from mother,
To offer token of love to the neighbor!
Her Inspiration evolved with a spirit,
To convey an affection from my heart!
She, who was glamorous in the society,
Lived normal life with great popularity!
If my dream wishes in future come true,
Certainly it will be in her delicate brew.

28
A devastated Island

He, who found hope-,
In the sailor and traveler,
Expecting to get a-
Reflected light in his career!
Though this island-
Badly devastated but alive,
He feels to live without –
Frustration but with his wife!

29

Sorrow and Joy

When nature create happiness,
It inspires me with good feeling.
When sun raises flower blossoms,
It creates environmental dream.
Happiness arise from my heart,
Which only gives me solace?
When a dark cloud moves away,
I never let the time ruin the day.
I like to appear in good manner,
Try to cheer with nice behavior.
I know very few persons in life,
Who share the sorrows and joy!

30

A Fantastic Cheer

It was surely a delightful-
Environment as none could forget,
Because my beautiful child-
Was born on that delightful night!
My heart gains warmth and
Everyone was in a fantastic cheer

31

Gentle Affair

His behavior was very strange,
Though words not yet change.
Once he offered hopeful hand,
I will engrave it into my mind.
In every blissful environment,
We shared pleasurable moment.
When he uttered a word of cheer,
Never fail to dry my falling tear.
A smile always makes me glow,
As gentle affair seemed to blow!

32

Our Mistake

Most of us-
Hesitate to confess our mistakes.
We always fuss-
But reluctant to express regret!
As positive-
Attitude able to achieve satisfaction!
The negative -
Attitude unable to bring perfection!

33

My Mother

My dear Mother,
You had been-
Carefully laid under the palm tree,
After half century-
On an auspicious day you became free.
As freedom-
Has lot of importance for individual,
Every generation-
Has to choose pleasure in its credential!
Your soul might-
Have flown from an Island to a hermit,
Then you walked-
Towards crowded place to stay forever!
Obviously the-
Freedom has powerful implications,
Which creates an-
Eternal and spiritual satisfactions!
Just one or two-
Generations ago, life was different,
But in this new-
Environment life is an adjustment.

34

Festival of spring

Though the color-
Changes with the morning light,
It shines out and
Developed gradually bright!
When people-
Throw their color at each other,
Then festival of spring
Brightly illuminates the slumberous night.

35

Fragrance

As the sun unable to lose his real brightness,
A pilgrim journey also gives true happiness.
Though nothing is doomed in the ignorance,
But life may be for all everlasting fragrance.

36

A Privilege

To acquire wealth one need knowledge,
As beggar praying to acquire privilege!
People who take a sumptuous dinner,
In the short period they became poor.
Glory in a situation of confused person,
Give happiness to a person in a situation of privilege.

37

A Joyous Environment

A sensation was born in my soft heart,
It may be love, not dream in daylight.
It gave me a very joyous environment,
Which glued softly in innocent heart?
When I cross from shore to the shore'
I smelled scant of flowers from water.
When his images arrived to my eyes,
I could reveal a sensation under sky.

38

Glory of God

O Lord Shiva,
   I sing the glory of you-
   You are beyond Maya!
   Marriage gives pretext.
O my Lord,
   You are supreme bliss-
   Lead to justify action-
Show light from darkness.

39

Beauty of the Moon

O lord,
  In this auspicious day, I would pray you,
Though there are many ways to reach you.
 I always remember to please you all time,
  But it needs a calm atmosphere to search.
 In darkness, sometimes feel sudden fright,
 As if cloud shadowed beauty of the moon.

40

A Vast Land

In an area of a vast grassland,
Forget all race think for friend.
To crate situation laissez-faire,
Carefully think for your future.
As minds blossomed into love,
It will give a solace like a dove.
If beautiful flower is swaying,
The butterfly will be rejoicing.

41

Mother's Word

In heartfelt situation of mind,
I too left everything behind.
I could hear breathing of heart,
But it trembled in moonlight.
As this message shivers spine,
I use to laugh, sang, keep moan.
I could recollect words of mother,
Who used to guide me for future!

42

St. Valentine Day

I was unknown-
About St. Valentine day,
Obviously felt cheerful, when-
I could find its clue and way.
In the Valentine day also-
Is the pairing day of birds?
In the season autumns –
Bird's breeding commences.
Let me thank to St. Valentine day,
Lovers rejoice and share the blessings.

43

Season's Greetings

When cold winds are blowing in winter,
The sunrays also scattered everywhere.
As we are exchanging season's greetings,
We try to share lot of love and blessings.

44
Blessing of Nature

In the gentle blowing breeze of autumn,
It was cheerful all around after the rain.
In delightful atmosphere of evening air,
It was treasure like the beautiful nature.
A thought arises in my innocent mind,
When sun appears and mother smiled.
It was really treasure of wonderful feeling,
When scent of flower is also spreading!
It was a happy day for my life's pleasure,
These blessings are wonder of the nature.

45
A Stranger

When the sun is setting the color is enduring,
Atmosphere is alluring as monsoon changing.
In the charming environment of the drizzle,
The village maidens are comfortably dancing.
In twinkle of mischief in his affectionate eyes,
I used to spend a few moments like a stranger.
In a beautiful and nice weather of this spring,
For incomparable guy I was eagerly waiting.

46

Shattered Dream

O Longing heart,
Don't torment me, move gently,
It's my ill fate as all now oscillate.
My mind sears in every moment,
Even all happy dreams shattered.
I wished for flower but got thorn,
Because dream of happiness ruin.

47

A Feeling of Nature

It was an early morning, and the sun was emerging.
It was a day of charming, monsoon brought feeling.
When eyes caught sparkling, it was lightening.
The breeze was blowing, the clouds were moving.
As thunder was appearing, the rain was just pouring.
In a few moments later, I realized no comfort.

48

The Feelings

O Moon, the traveler of Night!
What was my actual fault?
The lamp of light I will lit,
But words stopped in my lips!

O beautiful sight spread all over,
As my butterfly flew and flew!
My heart is burning by separation.
Because, I was waiting since ages!

O Lord, why she flew away?
I remember everything about her.
When I saw her in the festival,
Erratically she burns my heart.
Hearing her call I was puzzling,
When I met her in a riverside!

49

Guidance

I believe in Almighty,
Who will guide me truly?
I am thankful to God,
As He helps us free of all pain.
I seek co-operation,
Though may not be great factors,
I assure that all desire
Will be fulfilled by my ancestors!
Don't be joyless in
The house, feel for solution,
Always try to spread
Move in all the direction!
If things went wrong,
In-spite of being friendly,
Sorry, if I have done
Some-thing wrong exactly!

50
Fragrance of Morning

Wind was smoothly blowing,
The peasants were moving,
Sun was slowly emerging,
The cock bird was calling,
Flowers were blossoming,
Migrant birds were fling,
The temple bells shrilling,
The cattle were gazing,
Devotees were chanting,
The students were reading,
The radio was commenting,
The sportsmen were jogging,
Some shops were opening,
In the fragrance of morning!

51

Blessings

The flowers will give you the fragrance,
Let the Almighty give you all happiness.
The emerging sun will give you the light.
Try to concentrate on your good works.
May bring your life like beauty of roses,
We all pray to God to fulfill your wishes.
Though I cannot give you anything now,
Almighty will certainly give you something.

52

Karua-Chowth

It's auspicious festival of Karua-chowth Day!
And must be enthusiastic and the glorious day,
The motherland awoke with the focus of light,
People celebrated the festival in hearty delight.
To all the people it is a momentous occasion,
And it's truly significant to religious person.
Let it bless each married women,
The remembrances of nuptial bonds.

53

Lotus Flower

I sat near plantation of lotus flower,
It produces magnificent light over.
Some time feel cheerless & rest-less,
As if life without mother is life-less.
My memories of mother's affection,
I always feel a great satisfaction.
It may be the blessings of ancestors,
Even twisting thing never feels torture.
I never judge the people negatively,
As everyone love me very intensely.
I make friend out of helping nature,
Because I fond of worldly pleasure!
Let my lotus sprinkle in fragrance,
I will love its beauty in presence.

54

The Inner Peace

He who always believes in God,
Always puts trust into Almighty.
He who was hated by someone,
Never ridicules to anyone.
He feels delight and satisfaction,
When chanting good composition.
His soul craving for something,
When he comfortably singing.
He, who receives a musical piece,
Used to get utmost inner peace.

55

Innocent Heart

When spring come, every leaf swaying,
I feel every blossomed flower inspiring.
When a cloud of fine hair blew my eyes,
Someone appeared like perfect magician.
When love conquered my innocent heart,
The sweet look perhaps killed from afar.

56

A Peaceful Solution

Conflicts due to personal style if increases,
Happiness and trust will certainly decease.
I had a great ambition to be in paradise,

Sudden summer trip made me to realize.

Aging is the most critical factor to solve,

The new generation may not like to involve.

I had emphasized on a peaceful solutions,
The situation needed focus with inspiration.
Difficult to control tough & tedious situation,
But everyone can concentrate to get satisfaction.

57

A Feeling

In the beginning of my old life!
I used to weep in my deep sleep,
Though I couldn't control emotion,
Latter overcome with earnestness.

58

Cloud of Grief

O, cloud of grief! Go away from my life,
What should I do with this life now?
I can't forget those days that destiny plays,
Because flower don't bloom in our garden!
I became a cloud like the darkness of grief,
Nobody could fathom my innocent heart.
Now my all feeling remains in my heart,
Because my ship of desire suddenly sink!

59

A Broker

I was dematerialized my all share,
As I could not search any good broker!
I carried all shares to bank on a winter,
For lack of courage though it were!
In the twilight of my uncertain career,
Ups and downs of stock seen on computer!

60

A Fabulous Face

It was an auspicious stilly night,
When my memories brought light?
In the situation of foggy weather,
We both used to mingle together.
Love of enthusiasm when shown,
Seemed surprisingly it has gone!
In a peculiar period she departed,
As if garlands also became dead.
My cheerful heart badly broken,
For all memories she had spoken.
Her face was looking like moon,
But I used to wait to meet her again.

61

An Environment

My dad who-
Spent his summer at my residence,
Found himself-
Happy and with great confidence!
When he used to-
Return his native place in winter,
He felt blissful-
Environment at home is greater.
He who achieved-
Positively mental preparedness,
It was due his
Self-discipline and consciousness!
To get rid of -
Peculiar smoking of cigarettes,
Surprisingly it took-
Half century who truly regrets.
Though situation-
It was like a magnificent riddle,
But to remove this-
Bad habit it becomes critical.

62

Operation Magic

It was really an unbearable pain,
Because Dr. urgently pushed saline!
Though God created own image,
Sickness is due to eating & change!
I felt the Hospital was reasonable,
Where efficient doctors were available!
It was extremely cold winter evening,
Though I got relief in the surrounding!
As it was like magnificent playground,
Which created by migrated bird's sound?
A nurse who was soft but looked gigantic,
She was watching operation magic.

63

A Sweet Smile

I don't have your contact number,
Recollecting your smile with fear!
We met on a cold but a bright day,
Your voice like breeze blows away.

64

Bliss in Life

My old life-
May not be a bar for my sweet heart,
Because in —
The sixty also she remains on alert.
Though in an-
Ageing sickness suddenly can't find,
But it would be-
Heart breaking to leave wife behind!
When I sat lonely-
My spouse, who came very silently,
Uttered sweetly-
'You are the most handsome wonderfully.'
Though with the-
Happiness or sadness our love lives,
But she always-
Feels, 'We have enjoyed the bliss.'

65

A Man of Exceptional Ability

A person was retired from his service,
But couldn't control particular talent!
He felt a strange discomfort in chest,
As his heart was in risk and need rest.
Though Siva is the God of destruction,
Yet he is the source of entire creation.
He put his mind and heart together,
But his concentration was in scatters.
Without the habits of his punctuality,
He was unable to do something in life!

66

A Pink Rose

If I meet my
Husband I will offer him a
Pink rose to keep in his heart.
As he offered me
A red rose to forget past, but
I dream of him each night!

67

A Vibrant Sense

When she was sitting in the prayer,
I realized rituals are dearer to her.
She was deeply influenced by Gita,
As her parents prayed to Ram-Sita!
She was enjoying beauty of ritual,
To her, music was nothing but critical.
Her sense of humor was truly better,
And her faith was purer than other!
When happiness echoes on her mind,
She chants god's name with a sound.

68

Love's Grace

When cold and heat embrace,
I also felt his true love's grace.
Monsoon rains, summer heats,
Nothing is sweet for heartbeat.

69

A Fragrant Life

It was the season-
Which was mostly changing?
Delightful were the moments-
But un-heartily she's neglecting.
Even though I-
Will not shed a tear for her,
It will be imperfect-
If I proceed with my tear!
It is sure when-
Time will be critical for her,
She would realize-
Rainbow cloud gives shower.
As our affairs-
Revealed guilty conscience,
Because maturity-
Needs utmost patience!
But it was like -
Cloud of fire, which vanished,
Unfortunately though-
A fragrant life had been finished.

70

Solitary Life

When I was feeling thunderous pain,
Seemed it was about to be heavy rain.
As stress &strain brought me silence!
Obviously I used to keep my patience.
When I used to live very solitary life,
Even I didn't forget my reliable wife.
I tend to push my painful memories,
Unconscious-mind revealed my agonies.
My friend who used to talk about service,
Advised that 'peace may bring peace'
To step-forward with purity of mind,
I could not forget my days left behind.
It might be significant influenced of wife.
When her soul too tremendously echoing.

71

I Wrote a Name

Once I wrote a name in the sand-
The heavy waves washed it away,
Who wrote name under the blue sky-
The wind also blew it away.

72

Happiness

I never feel despise to any one,
Nor I never differ with someone.
He, one has right to hate and fight,
Because his ideology is not right!
When I tortured for service gain,
None could feel my peculiar pain.
When loneliness showed life's fear,
I need mind's true consciousness,
Though never felt bad or scattered,
But I admit that my mind was in fear.

73

Beautiful Mind

Though my heart is sad,
Your smiles make me glad.
When you are hiding head,
I offer a rose, which is red.
I will relax if you are behind,
As you have beautiful mind.

74

An Injury

Though he was merciful and honest,
But he was unable to keep patient.
When his ambition was to harm us,
His ignorance kept him too joyous.
As passion and affection not obeyed,
He got injury on his heart and mind.

75

House Physician

My daughter-in-law,
Whose philosophy convinced us?
With her behavior my wife feels great joy.
She, who guide us like the specialist-,
Instruct every moment like house physician!

76

A Fresher

What has not been done-?
To go to extent of committing,
What ought to be done,
We are every-time omitting.
It was my starry-eyes-
Which set out to find a fresher?
But expectation laid me-
Although my golden college career.
Remained unaccepted due to-
Lack in knowledge of happening,
It required specially-
A fashionable status looking!
The first impression-
Of fresher believes in a cool life,
But her footsteps didn't-
Reach so as to be a good wife.
It is that she gets a-
Feeling of sheer insecurity,
I thought it would be a-
Burden beyond my ability!

77

An Old Pensioner

Once I woke up in early morning,
The sun all most was emerging.
All around were blossoming flowers,
Holi welcome aggressive summer,
I was in the emotion, forget notion,
My spouse arrived for conversation.
She expressed, 'Am I a caged bird?
Looked contemptuously like guard.
I felt the terrible twinge on looking,
It surely made un-believable feeling.
When I put paste of sandalwood,
No evilness as Holi signifies good.
We had been to the Chockfull River,
It suited to the jovial mood to her,
God who knew every smile and tears,
I felt pleasure being an old pensioner.

78

An Auspicious Place

My heart was eagerly searching,
As evolved a mysterious feeling.
I was longing for peace to find,
But not smart to be determined.
My desire evolved since tiny tot,
To visit Loknath baba's birth spot.
Sooner step into auspicious place,
Egoism vanish awareness replace.
Prayed my ancestors for the right,
They blessed with their inner light.
My dream lantern has been lit,
And kept inner lights burn bright!
The flame of my inner awareness,
Gathered with the great happiness!
Memories of Headmaster's faith,
That guides significant true path.
Association of friends is truthful,
Who complement elder respectful.
If friends breaks pleasant relation,
Good's path scatter by separation.

79

Rhythmic Verse

In a cloudy evening and winter,
I really fear to meet with you dear!
Sweet feeling attracted this boy,
As love may create the tear of joy!
Though I remain silence and sober,
But I like the rhythmic verse dear.

80

A Prayer

I begin the day with my prayers,
To fulfill my dream singing tears.
I love Lord higher than the stars,
And love flowers in the garden.
A spot in home temple of religion,
Is relaying fragrance of perfection?
The prayers are the voice of faith,
Memory of ancestor reveals truth.
Prayer fortifies the self-unseen,
And gains spiritual significance?
All memorandums truly pleasurable,
Which is renewing as memorable?

81

Youthful Charm

A vibrant girl who was singing,
Who was very attractive in looking?
I burst into tears on expression,
Compose song of her depression.
It revealed fantastic amusement,
And created melodic environment!
Her life style might full of tenses,
It was presumably pleasing sense.
The girl is a very beautiful creature,
She thinks of her past and future.
Situation was alluring excitation,
Which was beyond expectation?
She looks revivable intelligence,
But lost her charm and brilliance!
Her song has great significance,
And charm evolves in confidence.

82

Moon Light Hooter

I was sitting underneath mango tree;
and could see two birds were flying.
It spreads a fragrance of friendship,
sometime created good relationship.
I feel delightful and nice amusement,
My desire evolved in enlightenment.
It was fantastic situation in sunshine,
When walking gently and feeling fine.
It may be their honeymooning sector,
Or waiting for magical moonlit hooter.

83

Illumination of Light

When our baby will be on our lap,
We both will forget our illegal gap.
We must wait to warm up our soul,
As to illuminate light from candle!

84

A Partner

He was always penning when sits,

Feels comfortable on lounge suits!

He seeks blessings from ancestors,

Who also believes good astrologer.

His adoration to parent remarkable,

Who feels domestic responsible?

He has chosen like a dolly bird girl,

Always remains friendly and smile.

His spouse seems very good listener,

Who listened carefully like a learner?

He, who always lives a very pure life,

Certainly takes good care of his wife.

He speaks less sure more he heard,

Who likes his spouse like a lovebird?

He remains soothe, never in grimace,

Even realize his partner is competence.

A fragrance of bursting jasmine in air,

He felt delight to touch his wife's hair.

85

Great Patience

There was up and down affair of mine,
Though feeling delightful and sunshine!
I was enjoying with the iron reach food,
Even was feeling happy to board into boat.
When arrived Delhi, it was a critical period,
But memory of those ten years ago is vivid.
The situation to study computer science,
Obviously leads me to learn current affairs?
I lived in hermetic environment and care,
Even 'I had no time to stand and stare.'*
As I had lot of works in the day and night,
It was needed for proper guidance to fight.
An experience, which requires resilience,
To achieve goal also needs the confidence.
'Success is sure who dare and no negligence,'
I continued my writing with great patience.

86

Blessings of Goddess

My life was constructive emotion fantastically,
As every event arises in pleasure fortunately!
I desired to lead a glorious, triumphant carrier,
Though yet quite cheerful with sense of humor!
When sense of pleasure of epacris increases,
I was unable to anticipate as ability depresses!
An agony, tension vanished due to simplicity,
Now I feel fit with the blessings of Goddess.
My stress and strain all vanished positively,
Always I feel relaxed environment miraculously.
There was boundless joy and full satisfaction,
When I could complete building works nicely!

87

My Teenage Life

It was the actual period of my teenage,
When friends gave peace and happiness!
Though relation developed in its own right,
But teenage crushes the broken heart,
When it heaps up with the mental reaction,
It created frustration and depression.

88

Parent's Blessing

It is an eternal affection from my parents,
Which evolve my happiness and decent.
It was the beautiful full moon lit night,
While on a river we were enjoying sight.
The scenery was amazingly magnificent,
While watching realized heart's feeling.
The amusement was of great privilege,
When we reached our ancestor's village!
Though it was thunder and the dark night,
But my mother embraced me in delight.
When I was born, it was a nice moment,
My blooming eyes were really innocent.
While sleeping my mother used to sing,
The memories appear when recollecting.
To celebrate my happy birth day ceremony,
Mom arrived when everyone reached to enjoy.
When mom said 'Do not lose our confidence,'
Same time dad said, 'Always keep obedience,
Let your life be filled with fragrance of roses.
Wish you a bright future and all happiness.'

89

Control of Weakness

There was a most presumable moment,
When he reached to a nice environment!
Everything happens under stewardship,
But he remains as free as comradeship.
Though stress characterized by the faith,
God rescues him from emotional strength.
The attitude ensures the freedom of stress,
But it needs to control emotional weakness.
If stress is the diseases of modern time,
We need to control thoughts sometime.

90

I am Relaxed

We always very eager to mingle,
Not to remain anytime a single.
As mind truly needs break to fight,
So we should look every time bright.
As I am a firm believer of Almighty,
I convinced never to be in anxiety.
There was the period I felt sadness,
Now I am relaxed and feel happiness.

91

Problems of Eyes

My wife, who was confronted with problems of eyes,
She keeps breaking her illusion, but feeling very shy!
She, who witnessed many low phases in her long life,
I sympathized for pro-longed domestic trouble of her!
She, who had faced worse situation too for her family,
Now breaks down and sob for her dream silently.
As she was suffering from a great illusion very badly,
I lost my colorful days every moment un-fortunately.
I curse myself while watching her face very gloomy,
As it happened to miss our happy hour, even daily!
Although she always confirmed to share my feeling,
With patience and affection of which I was convincing!
We had peace comfortable situation in our old age,
But her eye illness miraculously depressed me always.
She, who never wanted her and the children to suffer,
During unhappiness we used to embarrass each other.

92

Morning Walk

Before sun rises one early morning,
With my best friend started walking.
Though we were in full good cheer,
But in cold winter we both felt fear.
It was beyond grasp of our thinking,
The old association gave more beauty.
In poor visibility in the foggy weather,
Our mind changed to return earlier!
A beautiful cow that started to low,
It was relaxing in porch of bungalow.
With heartfelt joy and mixed feeling,
We enjoyed on that quiet early morning.

93

Beauty of the visions

Watch the moving leaves and grains,
Bask in the beauty of these visions.
Moon can see as clouds moving up.
Cool breeze rusting through leaves.

94

An Innocent Smile

I have seen a beautiful girl fortunately,
She was looking happy miraculously.
Her eyes look charming and smiling,
As if beautiful with Diwali lightning!
It was actually a solitary environment,
For this girl I had nothing to comment.
As good look always reflect inner light,
I could not scrutinize her multiple talent.
It's difficult to believe in spiritual power,
She appeared, seems merciful mother.
Though I could observe her brilliant style,
But I cannot forget her innocent smile.

95

A Grievance

All the day and night, I used to wait for him,
But can't understand why he remains calm.
He, who loves me from the core of his heart,
Even never allow me to realize and wait!

96

God's Blessings

My son relinquished his hope to God,
And he used to recite blessings of Lord!
He reposed faith and trust in Almighty,
As kindling a light, is kin's inherited duty.
He, who is impatient to meet his kin,
Seek God's blessings being away from din.
Cheering achieved through sincere prayer,
It removes depression, sadness and despair.
He, who prayed to the universal God,
Remains blissful and ignored the caste.

97

A Migrated Bird

Once I was in the deep thought,
Truly I lost my present & past.
A pious dream enriched my mind,
Radiance of her face I could find.
When the moon smiled at night,
The waves of moon spread light.
Her success was flowing like water,
As if like migrated bird she sang better.

98

Great Satisfaction

During sprinkling
Conversation in a park,
It became a-
Nice environment to speak.
I was observing-
Some children were plying
It gives pleasure,-
Enthusiasm and focusing!
With delightful manner-
Some children were plying,
My mood changed-
Into happiness for playing!
It was exceptionally-
Impressed their affection,
Started surely to-
Play with great satisfaction.

99

A Subtle Life

When millions of memories appeared!
In the middle of chaos all had flooded.
It was not satisfaction through emotion,
She vanished from my heart peculiar way.
As her sari billowed out behind him,
It was like a large rolling mass of steam.
Though love like galaxies and had formed,
But the affection of love not yet crowned.
His life connected in the very subtle way,
But she flowed like a river and moved away.

100

The Delightful Essence

Two years before-
The circumstances was delightful,
For that eventful situation
To my almighty I am very grateful.
Environmental situations
One changes many things beyond expectations
But it can't change
The true essence of our affection

101

World is an Illusion

It's sure that-
I am unable to inspire,
But I believe in God-
Who will fulfill your desire?
It is true to say that-
Gita gives us satisfaction,
As it tells us, -
The 'world is an illusion.'
We are satisfied –
With our sense of responsibility,
And will illuminate by-
Giving comfort and beauty!

102

A Soothing Song

In a soothing song sung to send a child to sleep,
We hear echo of prayer song that touches to quick.
Truth moves heart for blissful reward to find,
It is best thought to inspire a suppressed mind.
It is sure that almighty is the Light of Lights,
We enjoy pure bliss to which sets us at right.

103

A Singer

In a big empty room under the dim blue light,
I could observe a singer, who sings every night,
The most ambitious person who enjoys the music,
Finds unable to recognize ancestor's business trick!

104

A Softhearted Guy

When I first met him at the bank of a river,
My heartbeat started beating since that year.
Though my life had been a long journey,
But never could I forget my sweet honey.
I have strong faith on a softhearted guy,
I never had predicted him a disloyal boy.
As he is the boy, who gave a ray of affection,
Which still exists as love without intention?
He wrote a letter to me with a goose-quill,
Which gave amusement and a nice thrill?

105

Winter Period

In the fragrance of winter evening,
The children fantastically playing!
Cattle returned from pasture for rest,
Migratory birds took shelter in nest.
Sooner the days are getting shorter,
Everyone realizes a period of winter.
Stars covered by haze, sky cloudier,
But nights gradually become colder.
The curtain of fog in a long distance,
Because dewdrop makes appearance!
In delightful evening winter sun sets,
Old buildings shine through the mists.
Though I removed all ill feelings of past,
But for child's heartbeat remain unheard.

106
We Lost Our Friends

We lost our friends, who were young and bright,
They used to encourage others and making best.
Tear trickle down for our friend's invaluable lives,
We can only console them, as they will back to us.
It is surprisingly a tremendous blow to our heart,
What is the career, if beautiful life of friends is lost?
This is a tremendous blow to our heart and soul.

107
My Relatives

It was really a fantastic journey on flight,
Though couldn't sleep throughout night,
After arrival at home I stood at the door,
Relative greeted me right from the shore.
I felt, myself is really person of innocence,
They enlighten my soul from darkness of ignorance.

108

Consciousnesses

Once I sat in the candlelight,
I thought of a boy of indolence.
Candle lit but it shares my joy,
As if it forms the image of a toy.
A peculiar message could bear,
But it was not happiness or tear.
Life is impossible without light,
To achieve goal it need to fight.
If God is in recess of our heart,
Consciousnesses need to create.

109

Domestic Problems

His affection-
Was like the sunbeam,
Like sandal-paste-
And even moonbeam!
His domestic-
Problems create a blow,
Though nights enjoyable-
Like a bundle of snow!

110

A housewarming

In this pleasurable environment of spring,
Guests will feel pleasure in housewarming.
Some invitees would be willingly praising,
But they might be predicting in a smiling.
Though different kinds of pleasure & pain,
But tidal waves made life fantastic, a ruin.
An experience of new joy and the goodness,
Would not make our devilling in happiness!
As there would be no sense to hate anyone,
But newcomers will certainly love everyone.

111

Affection

He was like sunlight on ripened grain,
Though I was like gentle autumn's rain.
He, who was like the star shone at night,
Even remained in quiet and took to flight.
In the early morning when sun was shinning,
He rushed to a lonely place for escaping.

112

Soaking in the Sun

It was the fragrance of winter season,

I went to grocery without reason,

While soaking in the sun!

Though it was a beautiful morning,

I could not enjoy while walking,

While soaking in the sun!

Though I realize the good environment,

Felt an uncomfortable confinement,

While soaking in the sun!

Once upon a time I had been a golfer,

Even loved to play the golf regular,

While soaking in the sun!

I preferred to relax for perfection'

Even visit a place for satisfaction,

While soaking in the sun!

113

A Middle-class Family

I was impressively enthusiastic of people,
As brought up freely but uncomfortable.
Though I grew up in middle-class family,
Love and creativity didn't arise favorably.
As some people hated me every moment,
It created critical situation in environment.
When poignant scene caught my affection,
I rushed to pilgrimage to get self-satisfaction.
O my Goddess, I am your innocent child,
Who seek everyday for sacred and the mild?
O mother of universe, guide us to be kind,
I pray to destroy my anger from the mind?

O mother, I beg for notable achievement,
Which need to maintain the environment?
O mother, bless me to sing endless glory,
To induce my subliminal mind like flurry!

114

He became Silent

He became silent when I spoke,
And his welled up tears broke.
Though my mind was kind & wise,
He already opened my bright eyes.
An exciting tension which I had got,
This had created problematic taunt.
On a gloomy evening when sun set,
I viewed with blinding eye at night.
The situation created nothing more,
When he left distressed mood I bore.

115

Collection of Pebbles

It was just love of an absolute affection,
As her blind behavior had perfection!
I was loitering beyond a pond's surface,
But emerged from a limited awareness!
Once I had been playing in some shore,
Only collected few pebbles nothing more!

116

Lost Happiness

Once I stood near the wavy river,
I tried to have a glimpse with tear.
I inched to her with keen query,
Like the enormous flowery tree!
Though made my way carefully,
She met me and spoke fluently.
She lived on fringe of our village,
But without accepting privilege!
She, who had smile on her nice face,
Lost happiness for the circumstance!

117

A Nice Lover

O Lord, what a relation we have-!
Hours of smiles and hours of tears!
She, who like to meet without fear,
Always like to incline a nice lover.

118

Unhappiness

I am living lonely and feeling sad,
As every attempt had feels bad.
As you lead somewhere playful,
But it made my life unsuccessful.
An amusement flickered in your eye,
While walking bid me goodbye!
Though tears had denied welling up,
But it disgraced me to follow up.
Though goal is a treasure of life,
Your glare intimated not to be wife.
As the life was like melodious songs!
But it needed to run a few furlongs.

119

A Lone Traveler

It is an amazement of morning view of this land,
But my mind recalled for beautiful Coral island.
When I was hearing cheerful murmur of people,
The clouds thickened in twilight looked harmful.
The weather and the amazing bank of the river,
Reminds a good environment to a lone traveler.

120

Learn a Lesson

It was the period full of fears,
In hopeless life shedding tears!
Recalling grief knew no bound,
Though it's not happily found!
She laughs heartily on birthday,
Which creates a wonderful way?
She's never been an indecent girl,
Who grew up, looked like a pearl.
As moon could lavish her light,
She creates situation as laureate.
It's unable to transcribe sadness,
As learnt a lesson of limitlessness!

121

Loneliness

My great loneliness created hardship,
Unexpectedly broke our relationship.
A sudden change in uphill of despair,
As honeybee drink honey from flower.
My hope and pleasure had diminished,
To get rid of desire though unblemished!

122

My Dream

To share the secret of my information,
I reserved my melancholic emotion.
Though life was full of terrific stress,
Somehow I could erase unhappiness.
I removed pains to achieve bold affair,
As if, behind a cloud the moon stares.
In heartbreaking situation like stream,
I could succeed to fulfill excited dream.

123

A Tradition

As tradition meets modernity,
We should fight for prosperity.
Let God bless us with education,
To improve in our good relation!
As Vedic chanting is essential,
So to avoid suspiciousness is vital.
Change bad feeling unanimously,
We must live in society truthfully.

124

Childhood Memories

It was well-disposed life in early morning,
Not like a mourning tree cries on evening.
Thinking for liberal-minded boy was a joy,
Because childhood memories me to enjoy.
Some time we had great time on each day,
But real enjoyment was on the Sunday.
We tried to start our beautiful life a new,
But painful career had covered with snow.
In enthusiastic situation I had no choose,
Like mindless all went as slow as tortoise.
Childhood memory recollects close friends,
As it's like beautiful dream to be justified!

125

Sunlight

On the sunrise you must see,
At all, in needs please call me.
In an atmosphere of vermilion,
I will wait for your expression.
A pleasurable reflection of sun
Certainly will give satisfaction!
If environment tears situation,
Sunlight will be giving affection.

126

Friends

I meet friends of different trends,
Some were good some were bad.
As in sorrow and joy they grew,
But I never forget them to adore.
Though time can destroy career,
But I pray for nice time in future.
I regard all the friends like trees,
As they also nature's living things.
When I had a phone call from them,
I feel happy and never remain mum.

127

A Sweet Moment

It was in Narayanpore-
When smilingly he was approaching,
On that sweet moment-
The moon also was coolly emerging.
It was season of autumn-
When we met in a Puja environment!
Though I was loitering-
But felt confinement on that moment.

128

An Unfortunate Love

It was a fantastic-
Environment in the raining,
Because the black-
Clouds in sky were gathering.
As all the villagers-
Were interestingly enjoying,
In odd moment an-
Adolescent was recollecting.
'As if her joyous life-
Was unfortunately vanishing!
But an unfortunate love-
Everyone wanted to refuse'.

129

A Creative Person

In the youth his energy was emerging,
Like beam of the sun all enlightening.
He, who is really a creative person,
Enhances beauty of the entire situation!
When flower of love blossomed in heart,
A flame of consciousness had also burst.

130

A Festival

The Makar Sankranti-
Turns away the darkness,
And inspires to begin-
With the light of God bless.
This day begins to be longer
And turns towards warming!
On this festive day birds-
And animals are well fed.
This festival reminds-
Us to learn to be unselfish,
Even to walk in the nice way-
We can find path of forgiveness

131

A Gloomy Girl

She offered love without fight!
Like the sky, her heart is wide.
I determined to choose firmly,
But it was not known her reality.
Her beauty really dazzled my heart,
But why she remains very gloomy?

132

A Magical Moment

When I saw the rays-
Of the sun in beautiful environment,
I could feel auspicious,
Fantastic and magical moment!
It is a place of worship-
To visit at the auspicious shrine!
With its wonderful wise-
Enlightened moment of inspiration,
My ecstasies, peaceful feeling-
Brought me the great satisfaction!

133

My Homeland

When he was close to me with cosmic feeling!
I felt it might be heaven, where I was loitering.
I sank into sleep but my heart-sought apology.
He continued instill different kinds of energy,
While rising I looked at the land behind pond,
But I could not identify my beloved's homeland!

134

Ring Ceremony

It was the ceremony of engagement,
Delights it me with nice environment?
It was magnificent and a jolly function,
Which pleased with great satisfaction?
Surprised me, as I was not expected it,
Miraculous it was, I dreamt.
Atmosphere was reflected wonderfully,
Gave an enjoyment fantastically?
It was a gathering for Ring ceremony,
Which was really a pleasurable harmony?
Children were delighted with juju songs,
Never minding to whom they belong.
I sought blessings eagerly from ancestor,
Who blessed and save me like protector.

135

Beautiful spring

When the koyal bird starts singing in the early dawn,
The mango trees would be blooming with its blossom.
The Mahua trees would be laden with fragrant flowers,
I would wake up welcoming beautiful spring sunshine.

136
The Journey of a Lady

Like a bird she was soaring in the sky,
But blissful environment made her shy.
Like a snow-white swan moves in river,
Sometimes yearning or swimming in water.
She, who made sound like bees in the tree,
Sometimes walking like dancing peacock.
Like a bird she flies in the boundless sky,
Who crosses the coastal area without shy?
As an ultimate seeker enjoys snow water,
Ultimately she reached to land of five rivers.
She, who prints name with pebble of beach,
Tried to over joy to find her in great grace!
It's an effect of sunshine on morning dew,
As she desired to travel in a hut of village!
It was a period prior to the Diwali festival,
Her soul boarded into ship to visit temple.
She commenced journey from river Karnafuli,
In a few years reached the river 'Hercules'.
She, who took re-birth at the Netherland,
Arrived to achieve glittering career and settle.

137

Past Career

The creation of feeling is worthwhile,
As an honest neighbor's blissful smile!
A true friendship remains surely forever,
As the love is long as Mississippi river!
I used to think for each one's future,
But I never regretted for my past career.
My teacher advises to forget the past,
As unpleasant thought makes me saddest!

138

A Conversation

As conversation was fantastically unnerved,
His utterance was like the bombastic word.
Though he knew everyone are truly right,
But circumstances created unknown fight.
She never knew what the actual fact was,
Though her eyes had the real foresight!
His manner was easy but his soul as steel,
With his strong faith and hope she could feel

139

The Desire

When observed through my visible eyes,
I could find she bowed down with shy.
She, who never slaved of circumstances,
Achieved all through her experiences!
Some kinds of penances may be inferior,
But the desire in her mind was superior.

140

A Nice Rose

When I was in the my class of nursery,
Teacher taught everything compulsory.
I considered school was like a nice rose,
But later realized everything is strange.
Really I have special sense and feature,
But I assumed friends would help for future.

141

Dreamt a Dream

It was a day of the rainbow light,
I dreamt a sweet dream at night,
The matter was badly confusing,
But interesting, never felt boring.
That revealed the glorious affairs,
As if butterfly flew to the flowers.

142

A New Situation

I could able to solve each solution,
If would come up in good position.
I like to be protected for helpless,
Like lamp shows way in darkness.
My ambition for new way of living,
Was like new situation for everything.

143

A Pathetic Situation

I suddenly became sad boy and I grew,
Recollecting resentful things as I knew!
I could remember my mom's situation,
She could unable to fulfill my ambition.
Sometimes I use to cry for loving mother,
But I have no words to deliver anyone.

144

A Pair of Dove

When the circumstances become a better,
The seriousness also may reduce further.
The goodtime may arrive on the long way,
When dark clouds moves with smile away.
My life was a full of fun and also challenge,
Gratitude goes to my aunty for her advice.
Stormy situation crated to disturb my mind,
Now we can live in peace like a pair of dove.

145

Beauty of Lotus

The surrounding becomes a lotus of paradise,
It revealed memories of my beautiful village.
The grass and flowers dancing in scanty wind,
I could see beauty of lotus floating on a pond.

146

A Goodbye

I would not erase-
Memories of your beautiful village,
I would not forget-
The Hospitability and all privileges!
I would not move-
From that island at simple goodbye,
I would remain-
Broken hearted with the tearful sigh!
As satiation comes-
After a sea of the great suffering,
I would always moving-
To remain alive and throbbing!

147

A Picnic

Nothing could do about unknown fate,
Our friendship is the rescue against odds.
Though my thought is old-fashioned,
But I am concerned about the friend.
As the winter gives a way to the spring,
This picnic really gives mind-blowing.

148

A Ritual

O, Goddess Durga-
I seek your blessings.
You are Vaishnav-devi-
Saraswati, Laxmi, Kali.
To perform the prayer-
Your guidance is essential.
While seeing rainbow-
Like bird I am feeling to fly.

149

An Invitation

I put the candle light-
In dinner under the moon,
With a happiness as-
Arranged you will arrive soon.
If you are looking-
For extra few hours to visit,
Then you must reach-
To the auspicious day as tourist!
I feel you will surely-
Accept my invitation on realization,
'As Singapore bazaar-
May be a shopkeeper's paradise!

150

A Pleasure

Though I had great desire to succeed,
But my feeling of joy was uncontrolled.
I forget completely my yesterday's fight.
It may be achievement of today's delight.

151

Solitary Environment

When sun rises-
The stars vanish and darkness retreat,
Then I like to have-
Brighten up imagine with full heart.
If key to success is –
The ability to wear the expensive cloth,
Then informal wear-
Like polo shirts is the vogue for health.
I was always true-
To my work for business understanding,
Because I am grateful-
To Almighty for his delighted blessing.
Every day I recite-
Bhagavad-Gita for my future guidance!
When I become uncertain-
The Almighty brings in confidence.
When I feel sometime-
Solitary environment at residence,
It become melancholy-
Situation due to parent's absence!

152

A Dream

Nothing like wedding,
To celebrate the joy in life,
Because it is a dream,
To live with lovely wife!
If spouse looks cheerful,
At the flower-filled garden,
I remain satisfied for-
Spouse who has no burden!

153

A Colorful House

While silently walking in this late morning,
We saw a colorful house, which is striking.
Seems the house is fragrant with flowers,
Where creativity of love arise everywhere!

154

Enlightenment

I was in a sensation of the great mystical,
Even was in nice and profound emotional.
It might feel an essence of a true science,
Which was unable to be realized on silence?
Even to define nature of the consciousness,
It was part of collectively a true awareness.
A demon Tripurasura killed by Lord Shiva,
In the Kartika Purnima desired dip in Ganga.
An environment brought a pleasure sanguine,
But spiritual person brings the peace genuine.
The honorable life might be truly magnificent,
But dedication needs to attain enlightenment.

155

Unknown Person

As if in the silence of midnight,
A guy was glancing in moonlit.
It made sad to listening his cry,
I consoled but he said goodbye.
Though he lived very far away,
But I decided to find his way.

156

Gloomy Smiling

It is true that first come love,
As we both gradually involved
When time came for wedding,
There will be happy gift giving.
When the husband in despair,
The wife must take nice care.
She must realized his feelings,
To get rid of a gloomy smiling!

157

Domestic Life

It was overcast in the morning,
But ended drizzle in the evening.
My language connected a heart,
A few words were hidden in the core of heart.
If ignorance is self-centeredness,
It created personal unhappiness.
As the suffering keeps me hunting,
My domestic life created something.

158

An Enthused Person

My mind was shining-
With a shimmering reflected light,
As if bearing with-
Flowers of small branch of plant!
As without enthusiasm-
Nothing will be the really achieved,
An enthused person-
Works toward goal for worth!
A joy without sorrow-
Or peace without pain or fear,
We don't always-
Realize what actually our desire.

159

Golden Daffodils

I wandered lonely as a cloud,
That floats on high over vales and hills,
When all at once I saw a crowed,
A host of golden daffodils,
Beside the lake, beneath the trees,
Fluttering and dancing in the breeze!

160

Laughter

Laughter removes all sorrow and pain,
It never restrain in any of a chain.
Ray of hope emerged in person's smile,
It removes frustration for a while.
Laughter brings the situation sunshine,
It creates a delightful environment.
A beautiful smile can heal the damage,
It spreads fragrances like the rose.

161

A Letter

It was the endless but not useless tear,
As storm came nearer created thunder!
Your single word comfort my all pain,
Because you are wayward beautician!
I never get wrong impression to smile,
Better not to be the heartless or cruel.
It will be comfortable to reduce my pain,
If you kindly write letter now and then!

162

Scant of Incense

When the cool autumn air is blowing,
My heartbeat evolve, I feel charming.
When air filled with scant of incense,
It gives delight for Ma's lustrous eyes.
When the times comes to offer prayer,
An environment of puja gives pleasure.

163

A Nice Atmosphere

Though your hints of smile is beautiful'
But now it isn't a time to coy or bashful.
My heartbeat immensely was hugging,
But the situation of my life is confusing.
Though you are the essence of beauty,
But I have to resume some special duty.
As you have shown most earnest desire,
Everything will settle in nice atmosphere.
Though I hesitate to take strong decision,
Truly, your vileness couldn't be forgotten.

164

A Perfect Life

It is a beautiful evening as my heart is flying,
I feel spring in my heart and joy in the mind.
There was moment when I was truly restless,
As environmental situation created rudeness!
As if he made my life difficult and hide secret,
But happiness and sorrow made life perfect.

165

A Loutish Girl

When he arrived in fragrance of the morning,
It was impossible for me to express anything
Though my eyes were waiting for that person,
But intoxicant eyes were feeling pain as thorn.
When I lay for a support against the pillow,
My heart used to beat like blacksmith's blow.
To break the bow of silent, I cried like cloud,
Now feels life taken fantastic turn in the end.
As every bud blossom into flower in garden,
I am longing for a happy time as loutish girl.

166

No Solvable Decision

In a time of misfortune, it brought diversity,
The confluence of ideas shaped my destiny.
I could see my future through a kaleidoscope,
All my prediction has vanished without a hope.
As in early stage, I did not had pleasurable life,
In the period of future also may be full of strife.
Though my time moves with a big obstruction,
I couldn't prepare to take any solvable decision.

167

The Jasmine Flower

If I would be the Jasmine flower,
I could envelop your house floor.
I remember fragrance of breath,
It has created anxiety henceforth.
I listened to music of the spring,
But my sorrow seems increasing.

168

Shadow from Mirror

We walked on the dense thrown,
It was like a fear of broken dream.
Emotionally burns innocent heart,
As if my nice dream has shattered.
Situation was like the hideous dream.
Like a Swan I would swim in the river.
He was throwing shadow from mirror,
Obviously I was waiting for stranger.

169

Fragrance in the Evening

I was wearing a beautiful gown.
And was sitting alone on my lawn,
I observed birds were returning.
It was fragrance in the evening.
There was a cloud-less climate,
I could see the flying bird's mate,
They were probably enjoying nature.
It was fragrance in the evening.

170
A Judgment

There is a misconception somewhere,
I feel solitude internally everywhere.
To contemplate creative thoughts for mind,
The author seeks solitary place to write.
Though self-realization is important for life,
It is nothing but self-interest for someone.
As someone is unable to live in solitariness,
He must prefer to live with men in happiness.
As man should pause himself to reflect spirits,
But it must be always judged by his merits.

171
The Guilty Mind

I am always getting up early in morning,
Like Olympic player vigorously running.
While running away to chase a butterfly,
I had a memory when she told me a lie.
About me I carry always some ill-nature,
It may be due to little impatient culture.
If the guilty mind reduces a great image,
Nothing is real good due to disadvantage.

172

Village Association

I am pleased, I feel happier;
As I will be wife of Landlord!
I am flying like a migrating bird,
I feel delight and never feel tired.
I feel amused for self-realization,
As I never create misconception.
Feel happy to marry my beloved,
My dream & enthusiasm is evolved.
My music, my tour and my work,
I will omit all to enjoy in the park.
I like solitary place & environment,
To survey work steadily with mind!
I am fond of village associations,
I like to associate with aspiration.

173

Riverside

O, Lord,
Why does he fly from my heart?
When I could see him in a festival,
Erratically he used to burns heart.
Since I met him in the riverside.

174

Child illness

The old lady who had a kind disposition,
Relaxed her mind to achieve satisfaction!
She created the magnificent environment,
Even changed her attitude on that moment!
She who felt joyous as root of life was deep,
But due to child's illness started to weep.

175

A Friend

My friend ascertained to my mind,
As the river flows into the ocean!
There are weaves in depth of love,
As problems each one has to solve.
I feel delight when he was advancing,
The sun is best seen during his rising.
Once he indicates this news in flash,
Nudge like tiny butterfly to unleash.
It was like a dream of science fiction,
My friend escaped with imagination.
I unable to reverence as not wrong place,
As if sun is moving through the space.

176

Life is a Bubble

It was beautiful summer evening;
And was a beautiful atmosphere!
It was a glorious evening for us,
The sun extended golden focus.
It was sweet and soothing hour,
Life has neither pains nor pleasure.
She feels life is the music sometime,
Or caged like bird for the fulltime!
She was looking young and fair,
As if, brightness falls from her face.
It was thrill of love and affection.
When sun was below the horizon!
I feel it was beautiful environment,
But we both sat in calm and silent.
If western music, a full time carrier,
It may be just a part time of affair.
Without the spouse life is a bubble,
Even sometimes become unsuitable.

177
Routine of Life

Really I felt extreme pleasure,
As it's like delightful newspaper!
While reading the beauty news,
I was pretending like electric fuse.
Influential books are the fiction.
A fickle memory is not perfection,
As high school days were happier,
Competition also was very similar.
My friend nudges like tinny boy,
Who was writing about the sky?
Like budding poet I had wrote,
The teacher appreciated as right.
One can't be brave, if life has pain,
But the courageous man can win.
Child can complete a life paragraph,
But routine of life must not be rough.

178

A Nice Girl

When I saw a lotus flower sprang up,
My inner enthusiasm was to step up!
Vividly remember a girl, who was telling,
God is present in the every living being.
I realized she would give me pleasure,
Even I understood to get legal advisor.
I love genius girl, who knows modeling,
Even she had the habits of paragliding.
Sometime she likes to go for snorkeling,
Even sometime she enjoys water biking.
I have been traveling abroad extensively,
But never saw such nice girl positively.

179

God's Bless

I had an experience of ragging in collage,
Which brought me the amazingly change.
My unconscious mind always was flowing,
As fire has the property of burning things!
To get always delight or more pleasure,
God provides pleasure beyond measure.

180

An Innocent Boy

In this evening I could visualize the sunset,
Because it is the universal truth and fact!
Though I was born like innocence boy,
Certainly I will try to go without kinsfolk.
Around me so many things had happened,
But nothing will accompany at the end.
Everything will be remaining my behind,
It is 'sinking feeling' nothing will be in mind.
My all the good deeds or all the evil works,
Surely and certainly will be spreading all over!

181

Inner Poetry

He, who was in romantic love with life,
Unable to feel inner poetry of his wife!
He was grateful for the moment of joy,
Anger outburst into tears rolled from eyes.
Though anger creates negative situation,
Yet he couldn't overcome bad emotion.

182

A Co-Pilot

It was an early morning,
I was longing for flying.
But sun not yet emerging,
I commenced by walking.

When at bridge crossing?
I saw co-pilot also waiting.
He held for further moving,
Because it might be raining!

As my enthusiasm vanishing,
The co-pilot was laughing.
I felt tremendous disgracing,
I initiated him to proceed.

Later realized he was testing,
Though winds were blowing!
When saw a crew working,
My eagerness was developing.

Like a soldier I started flying,
But co-pilot was embarrassing.

183

A Flower of Garden

I imagine your presence at night,
Meanwhile my eyes twinkle bright.
A happy memory is revealing right,
Though not wealthy but have heart!
You are sweetest flower of garden,
It is my choice to live in the heaven

184

Bliss in Soul

He had settled in a remote village,
As he was comfortable with privilege!
His trip for honeymoon has saved life,
Even persuasion was better of his career!
His thought was deeper than that of preacher,
As charming flowers lie on the surface!
He was always obedient to his parents,
His service for society was magnificent.
His mind towards society was lovely,
But village immersed in ocean suddenly.
His fantastic improvement and goal,
Made silence is ecstatic bliss in soul.

185

College Life

What has not been done-
To go to extent of committing,
What ought to be done-
We are every-time omitting.
It was my starry-eyes-
Which set out to a fresher?
An expectation of-
My college life reminds of tear.

186

Homeland

If a friend used to close with cosmic feeling.

I feel it might be heaven where I am living.

My friend desired to take me to my place,

Even used to give different kinds of advice!

While looking at a land behind the pond,

I could not identify beloved's homeland.

187

Playful Childhood

I would never forget those days,
As my playful childhood is lost!
I am now a lamp without fuel,
You are beloved how to tell all?
I will lit a lamp of light in temple,
But the words stopped in my lips!

188

A Wise Person

Though genius lady was little older,
She was not even mildly wiser.
She, who don't want to say the real,
May be tangible to various people!
She paralyzed the battle of will with fear,
Or her relatives may be of the same lair.
As if fear was the source of cruelty,
A wise person must pray for safety.

189

A Dream

I dreamt a nice dream in a moonlit night,
I was transported to moorings by freight.
It was the place behind a beautiful pond,
I saw in the pond a nice lotus blossomed.
It was delightful and attractive to looking,
As beams of the moon was brightly shining.
On prediction I felt an auspicious moment,
Which gave me pleasure and satisfaction?

While returning, old man was approaching;
Seemed the man blessed with thinking.
Though it might be kind of imagination,
But his presence communicated sensation.
On his disappearance I felt an amusement,
But sleep disappeared, awareness arose.

190

Cool Breeze

Watch the moving leaves and grains,
Bask in the beauty of these visions.
Moon can see as clouds moving up.
Cool breeze rusting through leaves.

191

God's Smile

I always valued to my poor family's pride,
The God came to me and maybe He smiled.
As if I remained seated on the bank of river,
The evening was setting and river was rising.
And somewhere in the puzzled atmosphere,
I lost my God, but remembering his smile.

192

Domestic Situation

My un-consciousness ruined a relation,
When anger exploded in strong reaction
Though there is nothing genuine in life,
Fearlessly I expressed my opinion,
Though anger caused mini-revolution,
It evolved due to a domestic situation.

193

Innocent's Voice

She, who like the moony teenager,
Seemed it was beginning of despair.
She had great desire to become wife,
But I had proceeded for business life.
These are certainly called hounding,
But these were not surly the stalking.
It was the love of her initial weakness,
Or an experience of innocent's voice.

194

Her Presence

She's about to complete forty-five years,
Her memories remind me in great fears.
She spread the aroma of the cosmetic,
Though she is highly optimistic!
Unable to forget her fantastic inspiration,
Even her sparkling eyes and sensation!
I treasured beloved the memory of every day,
Specially recollect those on a festival-day.
Life goes on but there remains emptiness,
Every day was haunting us with her presence.

195
A Diamond Ring

I have no desire for an endless fortune,
But to find way of staying for-ever sanguine.
My condition was getting worse, not better,
How could be sure, great change would be near?
We always hoped for our son's consciousness.
When gave diamond ring with happiness.
It was most significant and inspiring to us.
His way of feeling and thinking were courageous.
It was a dream when offered me a golden ring,
I felt colorful sun set, during my glorious aging.

196
Morning Talk

I could see white mist over green hill,
As if it moves like clouds in the sky!
With the smell of morning dewdrop,
I met friend who wonders in garden.
He was drying the tears of his eyes,
But I could try to continue to talk.

197

Just a Friend

I had never dreamt about her,
She has been just a friend to me-
But now the things has changed,
She has become special to me-
Life at times was painful
But sometimes it's easier to say-
Without her life I would be silence.

198

Lonely Tears

The memories of pristine youth,
Laced with fairyland!
Now the solitude of heart covered,
Through my lonely tears!
The smile on my face greets you,
I could absorb the shock.

The end of part I

Part II

Contents

1

My Mother

My mom was visionary but a woman of action,
From whom I always derived my inspiration,
She was my source of big strength and light,
Her demise took away all my strength to fight.
For all passing days, I missed mom's presence,
I can't but remember her radiant & smiling face.
Her loving memories always calls me to proceed,
In joy and sorrows still she inspires me indeed.
O my dear mom, why I miss you every moment?
Though your loving face keeps me always delight.

2

Pleasant Memory

I was an ex-soldier-
Who was resting underneath Banana tree?
A twinkling bright eye-
Revealed my joy, as then I was free.
While enjoying-
Beautiful environment spouse indicated
I would certainly-
Be writer or composer as she predicted.

3

An Island Boy

In an island in the Bay of Bengal,
Lived a boy with his all-
Arrived from an island,
The teenager found a ground to stand,
Studies started with initial determination.
But attained success with good appropriation.
Though extremely ambitious for education,
Unlucky he couldn't complete his graduation.
In Homoeopathy he created experience,
But couldn't go with though held a license.
Had solace only prior to retirement,
To begin with the new enlightenment.

4

Memory

The happiness, glory and comfort,
All depends on individual's effort.
Memory is the cabinet of imagination,
It's nothing but treasury of own reason.
As all relatives bind us in same treasury,
It's depending on the shared memory.

5

Blissful Life

He, who is enthusiastic-
About other's success,
Can lead a blissful life-
And may always remain in calmness!
He, who maintains-
A sense to keep vision clear!
Always remains
Free from the ego and the fear.

6

My Feelings

Almighty resides in our body, heart and mind,
My inner voice was always guiding me to find.
I believe in God, never lost my confidence,
Keeping my head always cool, as no negligence.
I never started my work with doubts, being feared,
Even if certain tricky situation also appeared!
If a man is penniless, though talent with multiple,
For unconsciousness is unable to laugh and smile!
A pivot decision I preferred prior to start my work,
As appears rain to adore sky with beauty remark.
I never disperse with the doctrine of others to be gain,
Accordingly, 'There is no victory without pain'.

7

Class Monitor

The boy who was-
Selected the class monitor,
All due to the-
Deep study in computer!
He, maintained-
His class always in silence,
He could because-
In duty he showed no negligence.
His patience-
Always we can remember,
Even all children-
Of classes loved him better.
When study of-
Important subject had focuses,
He impressed his –
Images with more consciousness
His teenage life-
Became very delightful,
All due to-
His study was proper and cheerful!

8

A Greeting

On this sunny summer day,

We wish you happy birth day.

Relationship is like a flower,

With its fragrance and nurture.

If environment is significant,

You will be more important.

Try to grasp your life essence,

Like beautiful rose with good sense.

Your life must be prosperous,

Be fresh aware and courageous.

Be active and obey your mother,

Always be obedient to your father.

Avoid melancholy and depression,

Be optimist and give brave expression.

In lamp pour oil of suffering,

Offer worship and God will keep it burning.

I live as dew on the clean mirror,

And keep pleasure but not horror.

My broken heart had a desire,

To meet all in glorious affair.

9

A Wise Man

He, who encourages,
To face all the confusions,
And proceed towards success-path,
Who gets light and won an illusion,
May be calling a wise person!
He, who attains,
The spirit of self-realization,
Always feels himself-
Bliss joy and satisfaction.

10

Smelling of Lilly

We are always very eager to mingle,
Not to remain anytime a single.
As mind and heart need break of fight,
I feel then was certain to look bright.
I am a firm believer of Almighty,
And convinced never to be in anxiety!
There was the period I felt sadness,
Now I am relaxed and feel happiness.
On your letter I feel smell of Lilly,
I enjoy your well being very delightfully.

11
A Birthday Greetings

We wish you a very cheerful birthday,
Let your fragrance spread every day.
You created environment pleasurable,
As attaining happiness is not impossible.
May your life be the fragrance of roses,
And reflect a beam of happiness.
Accept blessings with favorite flower,
Always wish you a bright future.
I was proud as you proceeded to Africa,
Even felt pleasure on your visit to America.
Wish you success in study in B'-management,
Which would lead you to reach your highest end.
Proceeding for special course to Boston,
I realize is surely your ancestor's ambition.
Always be successful life as the coronet,
Be business oriented and be in kind heart.
Hog-Kong gave an amusement at a glance.
Even it better than business trip in France;
To attend geological exhibition if creation,
Then it is the climax in life to visit London.
May god always give you lot of happiness,
And awake you with noble consciousness,
Preserve your dignity and all the qualities,
Let your affections bloom for our families.

12

A Daughter-in-law

Sooner a bahu enters -
Our home, the environment becomes sweet,
As she will be the-
Family guide, unpleasant will soon exit.
A daughter-in-law-
Always brings home, the good fortune,
And removes displeasure -
Of domestic environments very soon!

13

A Joyful Environment

I realized war is bitter truth to face,
Spare time was to pass drink and dance!
Through training in missile I took with interest,
Though found joy in launching rocket.

14

Tension Less

Before joining in service I was in tension,
For domestic disturbances it continued till pension.
In service period I was disturbed remarkably,
Anxiety for children's education, it happen generally.
Anxious and stressful life I had during aggression,
No curiosity needed only more determination.
I was preciously proud of works with inspiration,
Hoped it may bring conscience a full satisfaction.
It was due to consciousness and concentrations.
I was remarkably impressed with my dedications;
My merit service medal was my source of satisfaction,
And was credit at the age of my superannuation.
With my association of Air Force staff and affections,
I felt magnificent impression and benediction.
*There was a time getting angry due to emotions,
In old age a good feeling only and no fluctuations.
It is true I was in tension before getting pension,
But at the end, due to success I am a happy person.

15
A Gentleman

A gentleman who joint in the defence,
On retirement he lives with confidence.
He, who was an executive consultant,
Desired to emigrate for his betterment!
The gentleman, who was born in a village,
Traveled abroad for privilege!
He spent a lavish in the beach fantastically,
It is amusing to live in seashore gently.

16
An unknown person

An unknown person, who was intelligent,
Impressed me mostly with his literary talent.
I enjoyed my works in many functions;
He gave me of a complete clear-cut descriptions.
My desire was to adore the environment with beauty,
To clear the conflict, it was an effective duty.
If a person becomes completely ego depending,
My loss was his full reputations and good feeling.
As I anticipated his thoughtful behavior,
It was not delightful to start work earlier.
As all creatures are families of the God,
To unite all, the responsibility, falls on the old.

17

Thoughtful Feelings

Though it was overcast in the morning,
The day ended with drizzle in the evening.
He, who was a polite and good looking,
Resided at son's home without interfering.
The moments of suffering keep on haunting,
A panorama of domestic life gives enjoying!
In afternoon of life he was silently walking,
Strikingly colorful house was spellbinding.
His house, which is redolent with flower,
Beauty, love and creativity arose everywhere.

18

The Top Floor

The top Floor of building-
Was a marvelous finishing!
It gave immense pleasure
While I was in juice drinking!
The scenery of surroundings-
Looked fine and excellent,
Of course this amazed me-
With the nice environment!
Sitting on smooth bench-
I felt thrill and comfort.
Even never felt hermetic-
As park to me was like a resort!
I felt more delightful –
To see lotus with Tulsi plant!
Even felt energetic-
To pray to God with chant!

19

Comfortless

There was a difficult situation
When felt extreme frustration.
Thé inconvénient environnement,
Reduced prospect of future enlightenment!
As unable to full-fill the desire,
None helped me or to inspire.
When image was utterly miserable,
No inspirations are favorable.
My carrier scattered miraculously,
My adolescent life focused ungraciously.
Encouragement offered satisfaction,
When conveyed thanks with affection!

20

Weather

It was an early morning,

The sun was emerging,

It was a day of charming,

Monsoon brought feeling.

A face was nicely shining,

But my tooth was paining.

When eyes caught sparkling,

I observed the lightening.

The breeze was blowing,

The clouds were moving.

As the thunder was appearing,

The rain was just pouring.

It seemed season of raining,

Made our program changing!

In a few moments later,

I realized nothing was better.

As it would need a sweater,

Because there's feeling of winter!

21

God's Grace

I am a firm believer in Almighty,
Which convinces me not to be in anxiety?
When I saw bright cool moon shining,
I could realize God's grace pouring.

22

A Park

Usually we both went to park daily,
But it was very difficult to go early.
When the sun was rising very high,
We could see some kites flying in the sky.
There were various flowers in the garden,
But guards opened for watching at seven.
I was too eager for flowers to pluck,
But guards were sure to catch me by neck.
In ground, we could see some old men,
Who were doing exercises on that garden.
All these were thrilling and very pleasant,
In this climate, it was an entertainment.

23
A leisurely Life

In service I was a relentless soldier,
Lack of understanding but sense of horror.
An unending flow of drink at night,
Made the environment for delight.
After retire I have enough leisure,
I find atmosphere of pleasure.
I was craving for achievement.
Though it was far behind fulfillment,
I feel sometimes grim or glad,
But unable to find what makes me sad.
Happiness is the family environment;
I realize it the greatest achievement.
To get suitable and pleasurable thing,
Like a budding poet I am wondering.
Life is a journey on unknown path,
It brings happiness if ambition becomes truth.

24

A Cow-boy

In the cloudy environment,
I desire for entertainment.
It was on the bank of river,
Where eagerly I played guitar!
When sullen cloud covered the sky,
The trees under were leaving shy.
With the wind fast blowing,
The rain was vigorously rushing
A Cowboy was bravely coming,
He was laughing while returning.

25

A Budding Writer

I could not be a good writer,
Nor could be a communicator!
My writing style might be perfect,
But unable to express any fact!

26

A Fragrance of Sweet Evening

It was in the fragrance of beautiful evening,
When in lawn we started gossiping.
I got surprised for my spouse's expression,
When she talked of impotency of puja season.
A message for puja shrilled in telephone,
As if a great 'tide of affairs led to fortune'.
I congratulated members and puja's secretary,
For enthusiastic beginning of pujs's centenary.
The courage, sacrifice, bravery and dedication,
All developed an eagerness and satisfaction.
There would be vibrancy with nice merriment,
As *'Chandipath'* created good environment.
When happiness would give an aesthetic effect,
Surely its focus would be explicable and triumphant.
The blend of young and old would be joyous;
The inclusion of all would make it vivacious.
It is sure that 'Life always connotes giving',
Obviously it would glory more our receiving.
Though my intense desire always evolved!
But frustrations, grim, strain could not be solved;
I leapt with joy, felt enthusiastic and delightful,
When we assembled being fantastically successful.

27

A Bride and Bahu

Though bride and bahu both are better,
But I feel she will be like our daughter.
Truly speaking she may be bahu or bride,
But really she will act as domestic guide.
I feel amused when she moves on a car,
Even reflects her drizzling eyes little further.
Sooner a bahu enters it becomes a rite,
Unpleasant environment very soon exit.
A daughter-in-law at home is the good fortune,
Who removes displeasure of home soon.
She, who supports business development,
Keep peace in domestic environment,

28

Stormy Weather

Sudden rain and stormy wind;
Barred my eyes from everything to find!
With a great willpower I proceeded,
To find blissful home as I decided!
I ran with lightening speed of life,
To reach the happy place to catch my wife!
When met her with joyous greeting,
The stormy weather was still approaching.

29

A life Partner

Before selection
Of a suitable life partner,
Groom and bride
Must mingle together!
To cleanse fouls
Mind needs devotion to God,
Even delightful blend
Recount beauty of childhood.
When a bachelor
Arrived in colorful function,
Courageous bride
He finds for selection.
Though it needs
The grooms to be qualified,
But bride should
Also be adjustable and soft.
An age may not
Be a bar for matured couple,
Fabulous manner
Aren't as essential it to be simple.

30
Teeny-weeny

A teeny-weeny child-
Who has a painterly eye?
Unfortunately left-
Her painting just for shy,
When she was teeny-
Had a blaze of glory in music,
Which gave an ascending signal-
And it's really fantastic.
But ultimately-
She bent on generally study,
She was struggling for-
And to improve became very hardy.

31
My Song

O Lord---
Is there any greater blessing?
Than a joyous song to sing!
I want to offer her a present!
And the song will be my best agent.

32

Intense Love

I sat near plantation of lotus flower;
It produces magnificent light all over
Some time feel cheerless and rest-less,
As if life without mother is life-less.
Memorizing my mother's affection,
I feel sense of great satisfaction.
It may be the blessings of ancestors,
Even twisted thing never feel torture.
I never judge the people negatively,
As everyone loves me very intensely.
I make friends as I am of helping nature,
Sacrificing for others I feel worldly pleasure.
Let my lotus sprinkle fragrance,
One may acknowledge its beauteous presence.

33

I Believed in God

I believe in God, never lose my confidence,
Keeping my head cool without negligence.
I never disperse from the doctrine of others to gain,
Because, 'There is no victory without pain'!

34

A Glory of God

He, who deeply versed in understanding,
Create the knowledge of spiritual thing.
Though it was the age of great tension,
It created something greater than separation.
He who realized the glory of Almighty!
Evaporate fantastic egoism like charity.
It may be surely the silent factor of his age,
Or it may be the gift of God as privilege.
He who was moving towards retirement,
Always imagines about an ideal environment.
Once he was a compulsive exhibitionist,
On retirement he became a psychologist.
He, who was suffering from depressions,
Happiness brought with clear indications.
As his life has taken many twist and turn,
Experiences helped him with many milestones.

35

A Genius Lady

Though genius lady was little older,
She was not even mildly wiser.
She, who don't want to say the real,
May be tangible to various people
She paralyzed battle of will with fear,
And her relatives may be of the same lair.
As fear is the source of cruelty,
A wise person must pray for safety.

36

A Message

You may be thinking-why I am not calling;
It was problem of raining and tooth paining.
With new thoughts and the circumstances,
I feel eternal value in God consciousness.
Just as the sun makes lotus always bloom,
The children's presence vanishes a gloom.
A friend may be always under lot of stress,
Though never brings his tensions to surface.
I was very solitary, creative and introvert,
But outside myself have a bit twist!
Though struggling life has various faults.
It's like an ice cream to enjoy before it melts.

37

Past Life

I used to think always for a future,
But never regretted my past-life as career!
My teacher advised to forget the past,
Unpleasant thought surely begets unrest.

38

A Fulfillment

It's difficult to recognize an actual rebel,
As flower's blossoming none can compel.
He, who tried to join in higher education,
Could not afford for best due to situation.
It was like a nice ceremonial environment,
when I heard regarding his appointment.
He will proceed to Harvard University,
So, I was glad for his great achievement.
I feel now it become a magnificent gain,
For my pleasurable time to sit in solitude.
A study of advance business management,
As it was the marvelous achievement.
Axiom in software consultancy in Africa,
Awakes him for long journey to America.
As heart always ripples for ambitious son,
I was happy his excellent career in life.

39

Churlishness

Every person is born for perfection.
Even each soul can attain liberation.
There was a period to feel pleasant,
To attain perfection one needs environment.
Remove impurities do not play foul.
Avoid churlishness to achieve a goal.

40

A Music Lover

On main road saw a green card-holder,
Who was a music-lover, with a guitar.
While hearing his hit music to prolong,
On excitement humming the same song.
I realized in shade of a human rainbow,
The guy entertained all in the beauty show.
He could not achieve his schizophrenic dream,
But his specialty was like beauty cream.
When asked me about my writing habit,
In reply I said, 'Writing is to me God-gift.'
My attitude was enthusiastic and positive,
Being an aged I predicted dull and negative!
It was torrential rain and a flooding river,
He was afraid of lightening further and further.
As it was the traditional monsoon season,
This fearing situation can't be avoided by any person.
Though he loved to live like an honest human,
His life had an unexpected and strange turn.

41

An Imagination

I imagine your presence at night,
Meanwhile my eyes twinkle bright
A happy memory is revealing right,
Though not wealthy but have heart!
You are the sweetest flower of garden,
To choose you to live in the heaven

42

An Eternal Dream

I dreamt a nice dream in a moonlit night, As
I was transported to moorings by freight.
It was the place behind a beautiful pond,
I saw in the pond a nice Lotus blossomed.
It was delightful and attractive for looking,
As beams of the moon were brightly shining.
On prediction I felt an auspicious moment;
I went to see a pleasurable monument.
It reminded about my sweet mother-in law,
Where with rose flower stood my father-in-law.
It gave me surely pleasure and satisfaction,
When I reached in that favorable situation.
While crossing junction of the narrow street,
I felt a pleasurable vibration of my heart.
While returning an old man was approaching,
It seemed he blessed me with deep thinking.
Though it might be the kind of my imagination,
But his presence communicate a good sensation.
With his disappearance I felt string of rose,
But my sleep disappeared and awareness arose,
When he was close to me with cosmic feeling.
I felt it might be heaven where I was loitering.
I sank into sleep but my heart-sought apology.
He continued to instill different kinds of energy,
Waking I looked at the land behind pond,
But I could not identify my beloved homeland!

43

An Inner Peace

He who believes in God,
Always puts trust into Lord.
When He's who hated by someone,
He never ridicules anyone.
He feels enjoyable satisfaction,
When chanting good composition.
His soul craving for something,
When even comfortably singing.
He who receives a musical piece,
Gets always-utmost inner peace.

44

O Our Creator!

As mind is a flow of vibration,
It gives unpleasant sensation.
O Lord Siva safe guard us,
Bless us to prosper always.
Give light in our darkness, *
Bless us to overcome all sadness.
O our creator makes us joyful, #
Let our ill life be always blissful

45

Beyond Expectation

It was beyond my expectation,
And I never had frustration.
Life taken up with an anxiety,
Because of berates by security.
Though there was happiness.
It created mental nervousness.
When desired to walk with her,
At a dazzling speed left her car.
She anxiously felt delight,
Though unhappiness, I felt.

46

A Desire

When clouds are spreading all over,
Around the trees it would shower.
The lady, who had trust and courage,
Never hesitated in the sound thunderous,
It was revealed when she spoke smart.
As if actual love bloomed in her heart,
She, who looks like a beautiful moon,
Waiting to express her feelings soon.
The lady, who was a jolly good woman,
Determined to live nicely with her man!

47

Nice Partner

I feel I am very delightful,
As never feeling harmful.
I feel to make good friend,
With one having soundly mind?
I feel quite satisfaction,
May be for good education.
I realize that I am happier,
As I live with a nice partner.
My wife who looks vivacious,
Always act with a domestic focus.

48

A Soloist

She who has-
Unconsciously lost her heart,
Unable to recover-
Or becomes herself a soloist.
As garden of her life-
May be with barrenness,
She realized its not-
A favorable consciousness!
She who recently-
Has composed a melody song,
With her post modern-
Tune she revealed and sang.
She who always-
Favor present over the past,
Unable to find good-
But tried to look for lost heart!

49

A Reality

He who has-
Pervasive essence of image,
Certainly can-
Seek the reality of paradise.
He who searches
The Grace of God by heart,
In future he-
Will not neglect or ignore it.
He, who finds-
A treasure of the bliss after,
His attitudes-
Of thought change for better,
When his-
Consciousness soars higher,
He uses to feel-
Joyous with a great laughter!

50

A Relationship

As God wants-
To see a happy environment,
I too must have
Obedience to good commitment!
As blood enters
Through smooth path into strong heart,
Eventually I am
Enthusiastic to become very smart!
Rose is red hopefully,
But my heart always remain sad,
Only my grand-ma's smile-
Make me always gay and glad.
Now surely I am-
Charmingly better than ever,
Of course it's due to
My grandma's blessings for bright future!

51

Creative Inspiration

It was source of an inspiration of life,

Which emerged from dedication of his wife?

When his creativity was at its peak,

It was wishes co-operation, which he used to seek.

He enjoys professional success of great height,

It all was his wife's awareness to guide him to right.

She was behind the success of business,

Credit should go to his wife's smartness.

During load shedding while he sat with other,

Listened spouse's stories worth to remember!

Her memory stretched from real story,

Which's an ancient historical memory.

He, who sits nearby to listen chatty wife,

Received unexpected honor in life!

52

A Greeting

We wish you a happy and pleasant birthday,
Let fragrance of affection evolve everyday.
You will be a captain of our domestic house,
As like as computer's mysterious blue chip.
Though environment is like a melodious music,
Our paradoxical thought makes it volcanic.
Enjoy an environment in the lighted mood,
Maintain your health as magnificently good.
With affection sending fluorescent greeting,
Eternal happiness might nicely be emerging.

53

A Confidence

It was the strong will power and strength,
Which changed his life gave him great faith.
His faith can't be seen which is stronger,
As God never betrays devotee's prayer!
His poverty had given him strength to bear,
The great faith makes him ever stronger.

54

An Immortal Flavor

In gardens extremely colorful.
The aging mother,
Who looked happy and beautiful?
When left the village-
The situation was not blissful.
Initially we must-
Take care of child's future ambition,
But it was a mistake
To leave home at a critical situation!
Whatever be the-
Circumstances or occasion,
It was necessary-
To carry on our natural function!
Though we have-
The same thoughts to express,
Our choice and-
Vivid senses need compromise.
He who was-
Going through a bad phase,
Which really-
Indicated of things being worse!

55
A Celebratory Life

At youth his energy was emerging,
Surprisingly when beam of sun's enlightening!
He, who was really a creative person,
Enhanced beauty of the entire situation.
Though life is not esoteric but beauty,
Print her name on pebble with difficulty.
Though it was not blissful environment,
But root of our affair was important.
When flower of love blossomed in heart,
A flame of consciousness had also burs.

56

Ageing and Thinking

Do not invite your tension,
Nature will give relaxation.
Set your mind in a situation,
To be delighted with meditation!
Transmit vibration of anger,
Feel comfortable in danger.
Fruit eaten is the detoxifier,
Which keep mind healthier?
If to carry knowledge of future,
Age of 60 is right to retire.
Be careful about food to eat,
On retirement keep health fit

57

A Grievance

He, who expressed about concern of life,
Revealed loneliness and difficulties of wife!
When his life was on a serious situation,
He felt tremendously a sense of isolation.
While on conversation he said, 'I love wife.'
A verse of his wife's, 'without him no life.'
He, who eagerly waited patiently for nod,
His wife's devotion was to pray to God.
She, who was smart and not illiterate,
Could think somewhere to feel little private.

58

An Anxious Anger

My un-consciousness ruined a relation,
When my anger exploded in strong reaction
Though there was nothing genuine,
Only courageously I expressed my opinion,
Though anger caused mini-revolution,
It evolved due to a domestic situation.
He, who was in romantic love with life,
Unable to feel inner poetry of his wife!
He was grateful for the moment of joy,
Anger outburst into tears rolled from eyes.
Though anger creates negative situation,
Yet I could not overcome this bad emotion.

59

An Existing Moment

She's about to complete nineteen years,
When her memories she reminded in great fears.
She spread the aroma of cosmetic,
Even though she's ambitiously optimistic.
Unable to forget her fantastic inspiration,
Expressed in sparkling her eyes and sensation.
I treasure high the beloved memory of every day,
Specially recollect those on a festival-day.
She, who guided me every moment,
Had happy life in nice environment!
Life goes on but there remains emptiness,
Every day was remembering her presence.

60

A Beautiful Life

One needs to have control over emotions.
Though poets gaze there for inspirations,
He, who remains always extremely cool,
Obviously could lead a life beautiful.
If life is harder in perishable environment,
Let us not make it harder in excitement.

61

All Happens For Best

In crisis one should stay strong and positive,
As we can get everything on earth to achieve!
When life taking a shocking turns in the career,
We should not blink, tear or cry out of despair.
As the festival gives an opportunity to rejoice,
The meditation also can save one from malice.
If a devotee has favorite place of worship,
It will provide with nice spiritual relationship.
If we desire to achieve happiness from Lord,
We must keep an immense faith in our God.

62

A Gift

God sent a precious gift to each one's hand,
I realize friendship's to remain till the end.
As without heart it's difficult to survive,
So indeed we need forever relationship to live.

In the new environment do not forget,
Friendship will always remain in heart.
Sometimes marital front may give fear,
When horoscope promises delightful career!

63

A Mid-night Child

It was the enthusiastic and glorious day,
As it's the festival of Independence Day!
The motherland awoke with the focus of light!
As people celebrated the festival in hearty delight,
To the people it was a momentous occasion,
Which's truly significant to the newborn?
After awaiting millions of moments, later,
It came stroke of the mid-night hour.
Who's born on the day of Independence?
Would glow brightly for a normal penance!

64

A Good Culture

He, who believes in religion,
Certainly be a man of emotion
If feels boundary of happiness,
Surely never feel loneliness.
If one creates a good culture,
Truly would understand the future!
In a flamboyant lifestyle,
Let beauty of life is more fertile.

65

A Pathetic Way

My heart, which aches in sadness,
Secret tears flows for gloominess.
There's time when saw him smile,
The heartache hides all the while.
His presence was an inspiration,
Even his voice was a consolation.

66

Tuneful Memory

Sooner I clicked the mouse of computer,
I opened my suitable file 'lotus-flower.'
My mind had searched for a nice word,
To write the message, but it had lingered.
While hiding the unpleasant nervousness,
I wrote my inner thought with happiness.
I closed the past to realize my temperament,
With pleasant flash of the present!
To embrace any loss with due consciousness,
I think lack of love it creates nervousness.

67
A Distressing Event

It was an environmental movement,
That I had revealed an entertainment.
It was a melody of pain and pleasure,
I felt like gold ye are our treasure.
Like sun saw you in the east,
When we reached from far of the west.
It was fantastically miracle moment,
Which had created nice environment?
But my relatives are under great depression,
I lost my enthusiasm in the situation.

68
New Year Greeting

In the forth coming New Year's view,
Let blessings of heaven shower on you.
May the Year bring you glorious success?
Attain all joy of life with the god's bless.
I sought enlightenment on cloudy December night,
With cloud disappeared the glimmer turned to bright.
My discretion, thought and all the feeling,
May give you the strongest touch healing.

69

A Shining Mirror

May New Year be for all full of hope?
And may we be given strength to cope.
Thinking of my innocent grandchildren,
I like to maintain my mirror unbroken.
Without air service I can travel by bus,
Of my relationship none to forget us!
Though we are very far from each other,
It's essential to bridge distance forever.
We must be conscious of our environment,
Only then will be focused our judgment.
Grumbling leads to miserable situation,
We need to have our satisfactory vision.
Our motto would be 'Do your best' forever,
Common would be our aim and speak together.

70

An Illusion

It's sure that-
I am unable to inspire,
But I believe in God-
Who will fulfill your desire?
It is true to say-
Gita gives us satisfaction,
As it tells that, -
The 'world is an illusion.'
We are satisfied –
With our sense of responsibility,
And will illuminate you by-
Giving comfort and beauty!

71

Sense of Isolation

He, who expressed concern about life,
Revealed loneliness and difficulty with wife!
When his life was in a serious situation,
He felt tremendous sense of isolation.
While on conversation he said, 'I love my wife.'
A verse of his wife's, 'without him no life.'
He eagerly waited for wife's nod,
But his wife's devotion was to God.

72

Affection

When that lady looked bright,
I used to wear a suit of white.
Focus mind was her laughter.
When things went on better,
As I realized everything okay,
The lady loved to pray every-day.

73

A Loving Memory

It's rueful to complete forty-ninth year,
After my husband made his departure.
He spread delight and used cosmetic,
His motto in life was to be optimistic.
Unable to forget his fantastic inspiration,
Which enthused me with lovely sensation.
I treasure beloved memory every day,
Though specially recollect on festival-day.
He was my light to guide me every moment,
We spent happy life in nice environment.
Life goes on but emptiness remaining,
Every day I remember, feel his presence.

74

A Good Advisor

Every moment you live in my heart,
Due to your guidance I am still smart.
I never forget your encouragement,
Which energized me every moment?
Glowing confidence evolved further,
You blossomed like a good adviser,
Your inspirations was beverage of life,
As tune of flute inspires to survive!

75
Special Greetings

On the eve of your-
Auspicious birthday I'm sending these greetings,
Accept my blessing as-
Expressed in poem all my inner feelings.
I will light special candles –
On the important Ceremony of your birthday,
Which falls in between-
The puja and the festival of Dipawali day!
Hope you will accept-
It as token of love and my wishes must realize,
As enjoying in Singapore
Which is a shopkeeper's paradise.
I realize that bride
Or bahu equal and always better,
Because I always
Treat daughter-in-law as my lovely daughter.
Sooner a bahu enters
Into home, the environment's set at right,
As she will be-
The family guide, unpleasant will soon exit.
A daughter-in-law-
Always brings home, the good fortune,
And removes displeasure –
From domestic environments very soon!
Your support in business-
Cultivated the sense of responsibility,

Being a graduate and-
An MBA you assumed huge personality.
Though home will be-
The reflection of your suitable husband,
Let God bless you-
For magnificent decision of your mind!

76

A Neighbor Girl

She, who was a teenager of beauty,
Was none else, but my neighbor lady.
She behaved moonstruck teenager,
Seemed it was beginning of despair.
She threw herself into a great trouble,
Due to curliness felt it's impossible.
She had great desire to become wife,
But I had proceeded for a study life.
These are certainly called hounding,
But these were not surly the stalking.
It was the love of my initial weakness,
Or an experience of innocent's voice.

77

An Echo of Prayers

In a soothing song sung to send a child to sleep.
We hear the echo of prayer song that touches to quick.
Truth moves heart for blissful reward to find,
It is best thought to inspire a suppressed mind.
It is sure that almighty is the Light of Lights,
We enjoy pure bliss to which sets us at right.

78

Peacock Dancing

There was no-
Boundaries of my happiness,
Though I was-
In deep forest and felt loneliness?
As from a distance-
Happily I saw peacock dancing.
The rustle sound-
Of wind over trees was flowing.

79
Birthday Greeting

Wish you happy birthday,
Let God bless you this day.
He, who believes in religion,
Certainly feels a good emotion.
No boundary of happiness,
If you never feel loneliness,
You have created good culture,
Which indicate your bright future?
In your flamboyant lifestyle,
Let your life be more fertile.
As meditation gives awareness,
Always be in consciousness.

80

The Reminiscence

He had an excellent reminiscence,
He reminded of when he sat on solace.
He recollects fragrance of a rose flower,
When he reminisces memory of sweet lover!
Though sweet memory passes for a while,
He sometimes chuckles or gives smile.
Smile, laughter and sunshine are delightful,
So also life's sunset's magnificently beautiful.
He recollects his spouse, who sings in shy,
The old guy sees white clouds in the sky.
He has forgotten the thorns of rose,
As he is living always with his spouse!

81

A Flagship

What a flaming environment,
He is flagship in this moment.
With flamingo I like to sing,
A sweet environment to bring!

82

Eventful Circumstances

Two years before-
The circumstances was delightful,
For that eventful situation
To my almighty I am very grateful.
Environmental situations
One change many things beyond our expectation
But it can't change
The delightful essence of our affection!

83

A vision

Do not cloud your eyes in tears,
Better to keep your vision clear.
Make all personal nature sweet,
Surely future will remain bright.

84

An Indigenous Man

The land that-
The indigents desired to see,
Could not-
Focus even the glimpse of beauty.
He, who is-
Indigenous man of that island,
Carefully revealed-
Of his ancestor's activities and mind!
Though earlier-
He traveled to different place,
But it's the-
Native village where he lived in peace.

85

An Emotional Style

My mom, who joyfully adored Almighty,
Was pleasingly cleaver and talked smartly.
She, who had the grace through looked sheepish,
Created blissful environment to cherish!
Through the process of transformation,
She took various shapes like various birds.
She, who transformed the beam of a light,
As like a Kriya Yogi she used to sit straight.

86

Wind Bent Grasses

I was crossing the border of village,
When awarded an excellent privilege.
People valued us though were poor,
And I desired for a girl of the next door.
In our village saw the silent girl pass,
As I observed wind to bend grass!
She looked really very beautiful,
Sing her I felt immensely delightful.

87

A Great Foul

O, Lord your love aluminous my soul,
But situation made me play some foul.
As springs unable to forget the note of bird,
Your blessings on me I can't discard.

88

The Photographic Image

Inner energy gives me satisfactions.
And everything with me nicely functions,
I will always be with an apologetic mind;
When cause of throbbing pain I shall find!
Interval sometimes brought an end of talk,
But no break with her memories sulks.

89

Prayer

O My Almighty-
Your compassion truly limitless,
Let me enjoy give me happiness.
Help those who seek forgiveness,
Protect them from harms with thy kindness.

90

Pearly Wisdom

When observed through my visible eyes,
It seemed she bowed down with shy.
She, who's never a slaved of circumstances,
Achieved all through her experiences.
All kinds of penances are inferior,
When desires in a mind are superior.
If a man loves his ideas and possession,
Will never suffer from sorrows and tension!

91

Master's Advice

The creation of feeling is worthwhile,
On an honest neighbor's blissful smile!
A true friendship remains surely forever,
As the love is long as Mississippi river
I always think for each one's future,
Even I never regret for my career.
My Masters advises to forget the past,
As unpleasant thought makes me saddest!

92

A Heart of Guy

For every beauty there is an eye,
Somewhere we have to see it-
For love there is a heart of guy.
Somewhere she has to receive that.

93

On The Beach

She who looked
Very beautiful in the morning,
Desired to travel at
Beach in the fragrance of evening!

94

An Injury

Though he was merciful and honest,
It was uncomfortable to keep a patient.
Though his ambition was to harm us,
But ignorance kept him joyous.
As passion and affection not obeyed,
He got injury in his heart and in mind.

95

A Pleasure

I live as I please-
Even I feel always pleasure,
I move as I like-
Because my heart is clear.
I felt happiness-
When I visited this nice land,
It was like my native place
Which resample a beautiful island?
She also looked happy-
In the boat on the flowery river,
Her frame of mind
Was blossomed into flower!

96

A Magnificent Situation

The old lady, who had a kindly disposition,
Relaxed her mind to achieve satisfaction!
She created magnificent environment.
To change her mind on that moment!
She, who thought root of life, is deep.
But due to child's illness she had to weep.

97

Happiness

Laughter has the best tonic effect,

It reduces inner tension & conflict.

If desires to lead a glorious career,

He must be cheerful everywhere.

The sense of humor keeps me pleasant,

To take humor should not be hesitant.

He, who feels happiness of others,

It will be most fortunate forever.

If desires to recollect memories,

He will remain happiness even seventies.

98

An Inspiration

When I saw ray-
Of the sun in beautiful environment,
I felt auspiciously-
Of a fantastic and magical moment!
It was a place of worship-
For anyone visiting the shrine.
Birds completed prayer with chirp
With chant there arose the clime.
With it's wonderfully,-
Enlightened moment of inspiration,
My ecstasies peaceful-
Feeling brought me great satisfaction.

99

A Smile

For a while-
I could see your beautiful smile.
Let God make-
Your career always successful!
It was a pleasant-
Environment with the ray of the moon,
To responded to it-
We would be together very soon!
You are the-
Teenager and beautifully simple,
Needless to say-
You looked lovingly beautiful.

100

An Immense Joy

They, who were bright, highly educated,
Try to follow up for the career they bred.
They immersed in the joy of developing,
As the life was too short to worth living!
The Young were abandoning business,
It was due to lack of self-consciousness.
In the village there was magical silence,
We desired glass of egg with appliance.
He, who sipped first, left the print from lip,
As there was the glass to taste and sip!
In change of season with joys & worries,
We realized the thoughts, hope and tears.

101

A Sweet Feeling

She would not be partial in judgment,
For the culture and her environment.
She, who had abode by righteousness,
Let Lord induces in her consciousness.
I was crossing the border of this village,
But was awarded an excellent privilege.
Though we were magnificently poor,
I desired a girl of the next door.
When the same girl silently crossed,
As if pleasantly wind also bent the grass.
She, who looked really very beautiful,
I felt unimaginably delightful.

102

My Child

My joy I felt was a boundless,
As 'The sun rises to disperse darkness.'
When I held my new born baby on arms,
One can't imagine of my inner charms.
My thought and flexible feeling had a fear,
As if 'God Vishnu blessed to destroy error.'
I was a tyrant & insensitive in early stage,
Though it was insignificant in the middle age.
It became a mysterious feeling certainly,
When my child was eying on me very gently.
I believed in God though I can't define,
Yet appeared an illusion because of this child of mine.
It was miraculous and delightful when we smiled,
I prayed to God for healthier fortune of child.
'Happy is the man, who has a balanced mind,'
I determined to bring up a perfect child.
My dream, patience were never had been shattered,
Even never had diffidence, as I was so inspired.
I had faced worse though, though not retired,
On my retirement, he satisfied what we desired.

103

The Joy of Life

Nothing like wedding to celebrate the joy of life,
Though it is joy of dream to be with happy wife.
She looked cheerful like the flower-filled garden,
I too was satisfied with my spouse, who had no burden.

104

A Victory

It is a victory to become a writer,
I too was an enthusiast for earlier.
Ignorance brings self-centeredness,
And causes personal unhappiness.
My language connected two hearts,
Though some words remained hidden.
I who is a retired serviceman first,
Am leading my life surely towards sunset.
I recollect my childhood in evening,
Realize happiness while sleeping.

105
Speed Visit

It was true at first sight we loved,
And gradually got more and more involved.
At last the occasion came for gift giving,
As the time had come for our wedding.
Then time came for speed visiting,
As both desired a good trekking.

106
Source of Inspiration

I recollect dad's big source of inspiration,
I was unable to imagine his sane affection.
He was a cordial and hard working person,
To convey goodwill was his conscious mission.
Every day was a new day with new challenge,
As if to overcome with strength and courage!
He never pardoned distorting comments,
The distorting words might be from innocent!
Core of memories, the source of my happiness,
Till his old age I never found him ruthless.
His old age manners too were essential graceful,
Everybody around him was ever delightful.
His retired life was tender, needed more care,
Nothing less, than to honor his dream would be fair.

107

Worshiping

Once I was in a delighted mood,
My spiritual inspiration was good.
I was praying to Vivekananda swami,
When my enthusiastic friends called me.
I assumed it stopped my genius image,
So requested them to maintain my image.
It became unhealthy to convince,
As they would took it for my negligence.
My derogatory remarks opened their eyes,
Miraculously they vanished with shy.
Intelligently and tactfully all was solved,
As in it my confidence was involved.

108

A Pilgrim Journey

In the *Magha Purnima* morning,
We had great desire for travelling.
Started our journey to hilly place,
Enjoyed sight scenery at a glance!

Though sky was clear inky blue,
Peacocks were dancing for no clue.
When the cold winter reached,
It was delightful when our Ma blessed.
Surprisingly panda called for Prosad,
I stretched my hand and that I had.
Chill winter sky's quite clear,
And the successful journey gave us pleasure.

The End

Printed in the United States
By Bookmasters